ROCKFORD PUBLIC LIBRARY

3 1112 020304040

W9-AGH-686

WITHDRAWN

Kid Pick!

Title: _____

Author: _____

Picked by: _____

_____

Why I love this book:

_____

_____

ROCKFORD PUBLIC LIBRARY

Rockford, Illinois

www.rockfordpubliclibrary.org

815-965-9511

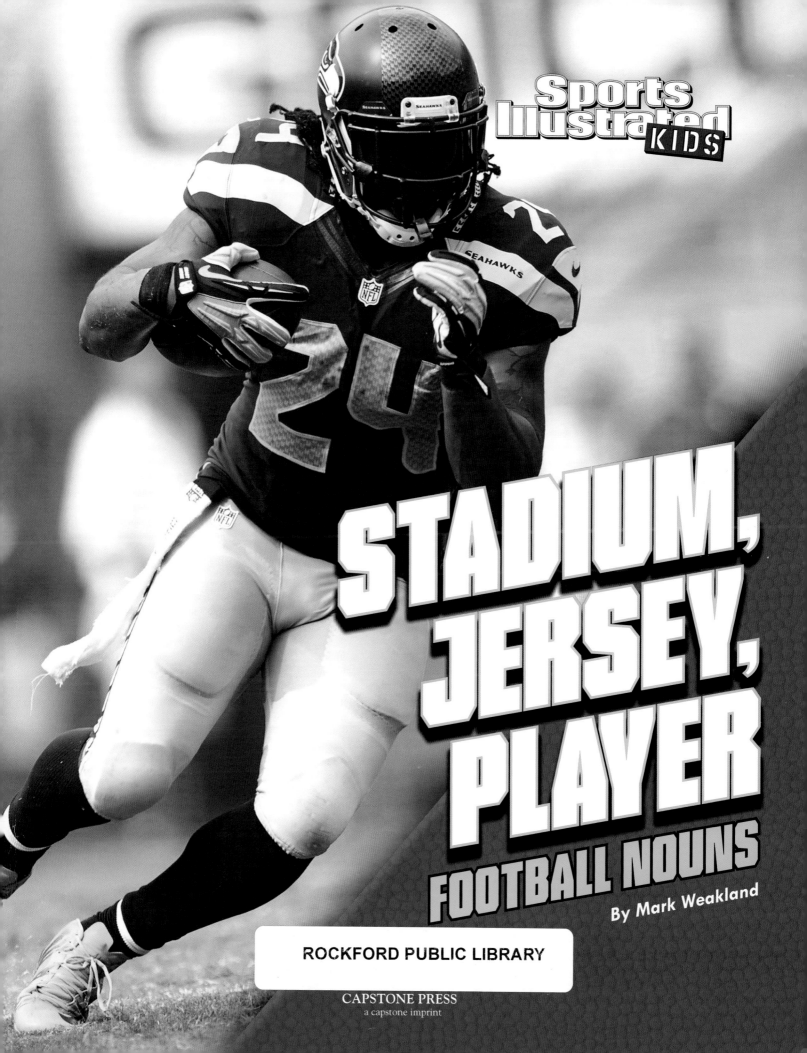

Sports Illustrated KIDS

STADIUM, JERSEY, PLAYER
FOOTBALL NOUNS

By Mark Weakland

ROCKFORD PUBLIC LIBRARY

CAPSTONE PRESS
a capstone imprint

The day for the big game has arrived, and football **nouns** are everywhere! A noun is a person, place, or thing. The football, the field, the fans—they are all nouns. Let's get the game started and find more football nouns!

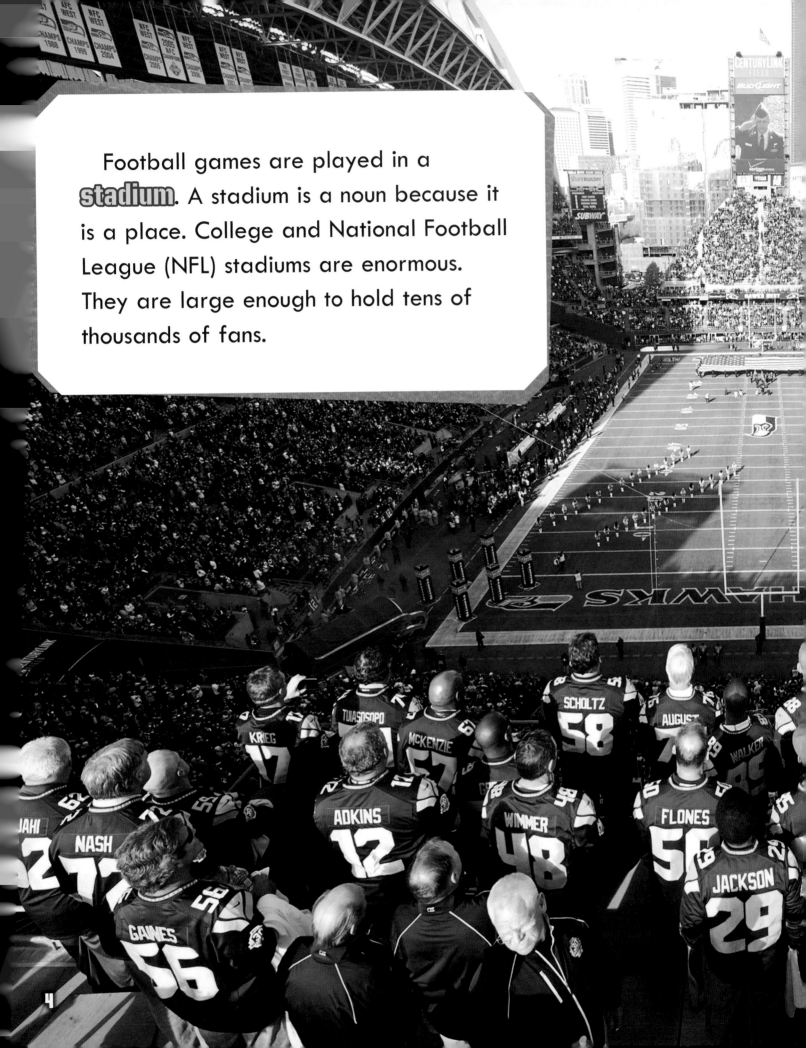

Football games are played in a **stadium**. A stadium is a noun because it is a place. College and National Football League (NFL) stadiums are enormous. They are large enough to hold tens of thousands of fans.

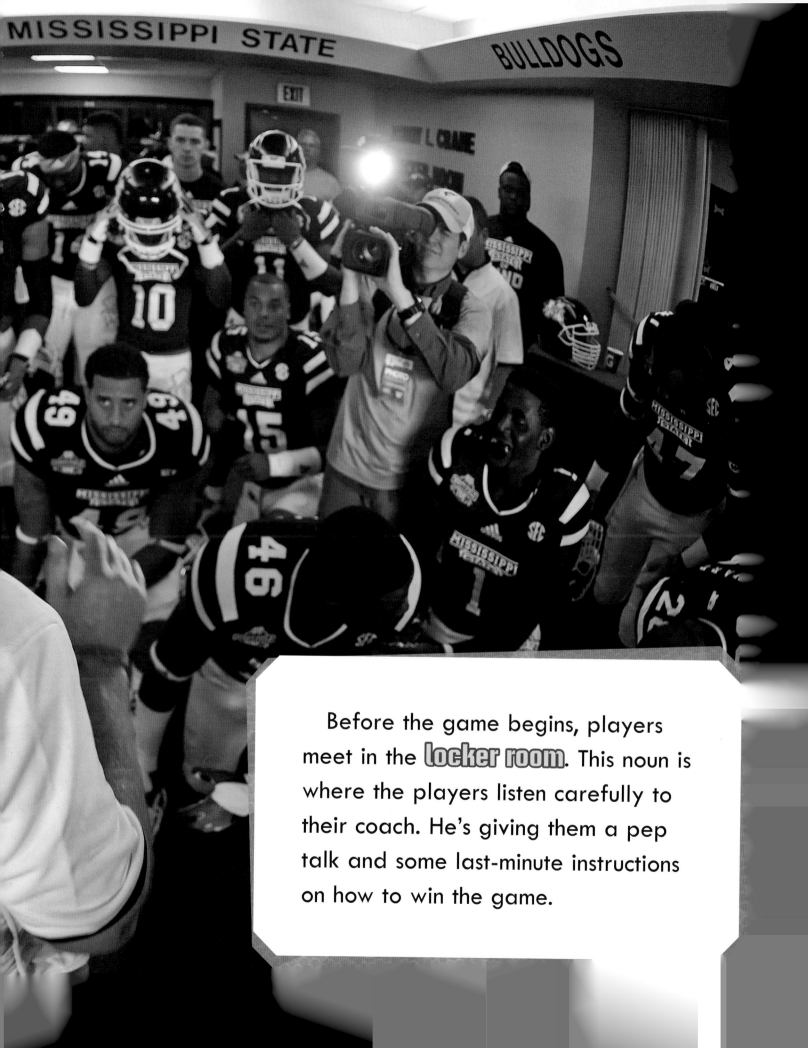

Before the game begins, players meet in the **locker room**. This noun is where the players listen carefully to their coach. He's giving them a pep talk and some last-minute instructions on how to win the game.

When the **players** and their **coach** rush onto the field, the **fans** go wild. Soon the game will start. Coaches, fans, and players are people, and people are nouns too. At a crowded football game, nouns pack the stadium!

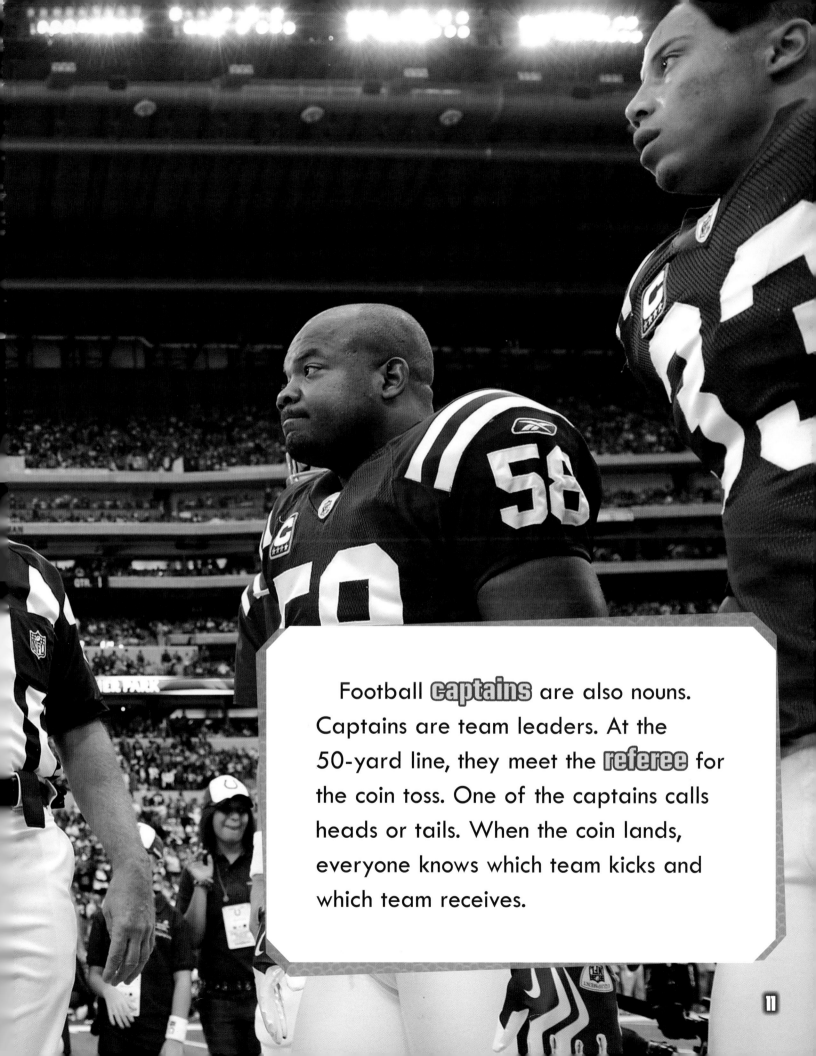

Football **captains** are also nouns. Captains are team leaders. At the 50-yard line, they meet the **referee** for the coin toss. One of the captains calls heads or tails. When the coin lands, everyone knows which team kicks and which team receives.

With a tremendous swing of his leg, the kicker boots the **football** off the **tee**. The game has begun! All things are nouns—a football, a tee, or even a player's sock! Can you name other nouns in this picture?

Equipment is a noun that helps protect football players from injuries. A **helmet** with a facemask and chinstrap protects a player's head. **Pads** keep his shoulders, chest, and thighs safe. **Gloves** and **wraps** guard his hands and arms.

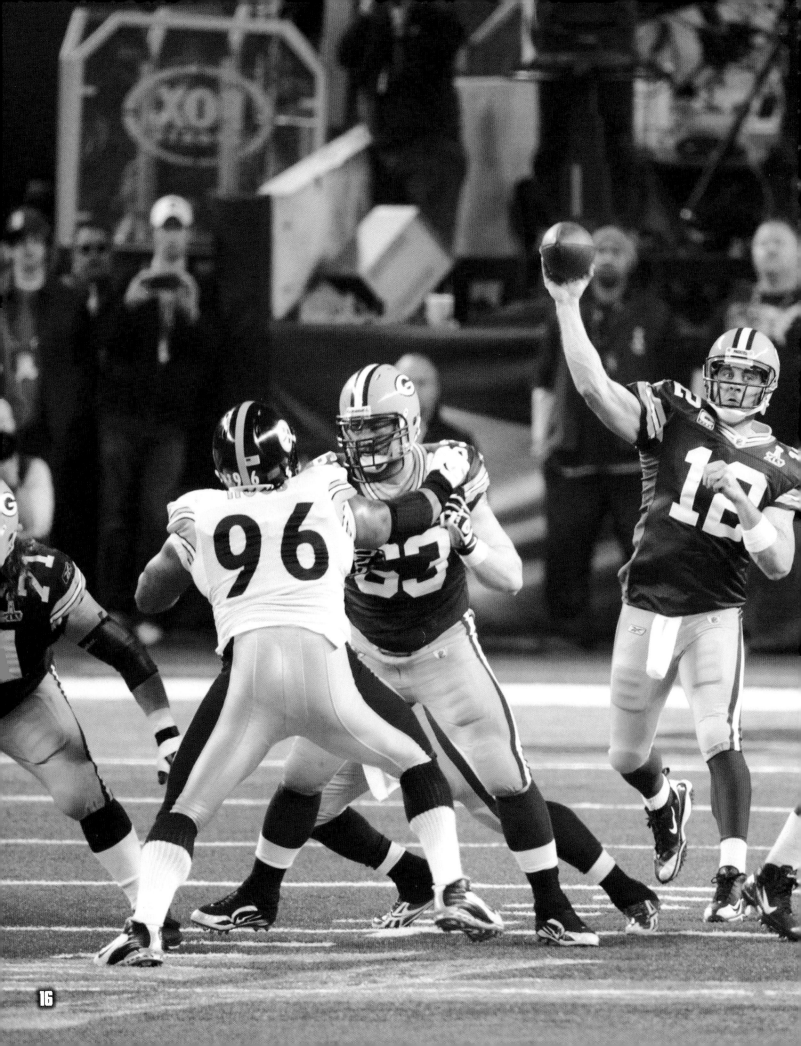

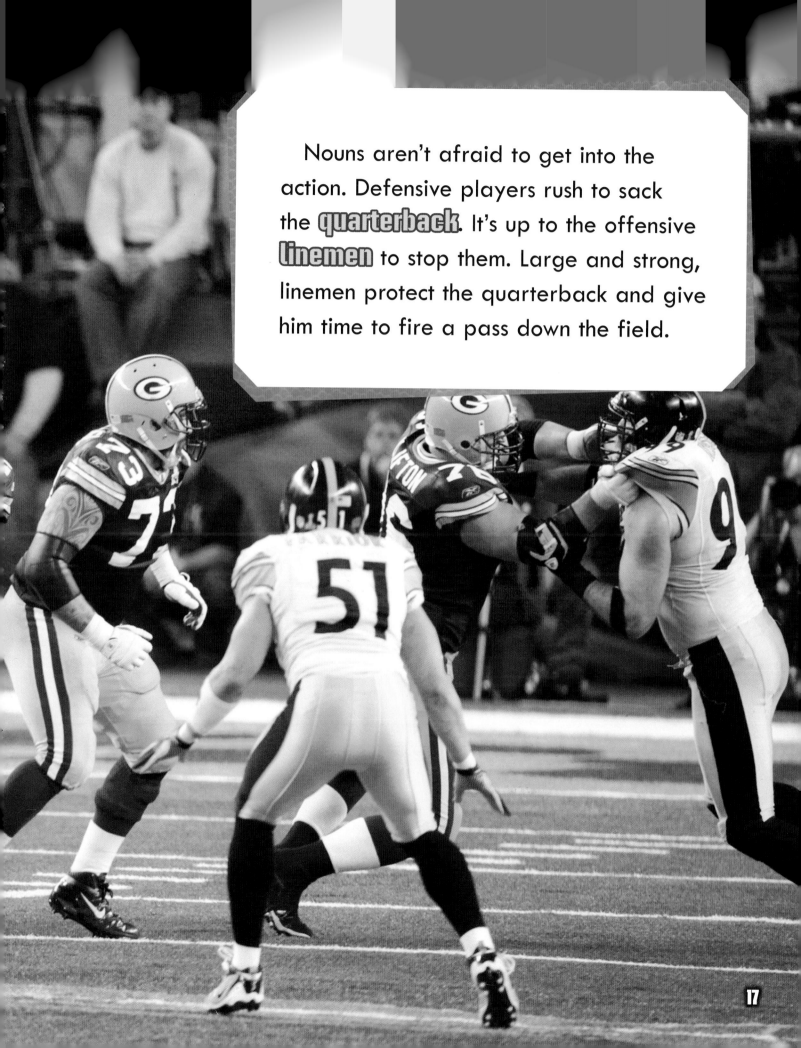

Nouns aren't afraid to get into the action. Defensive players rush to sack the **quarterback**. It's up to the offensive **linemen** to stop them. Large and strong, linemen protect the quarterback and give him time to fire a pass down the field.

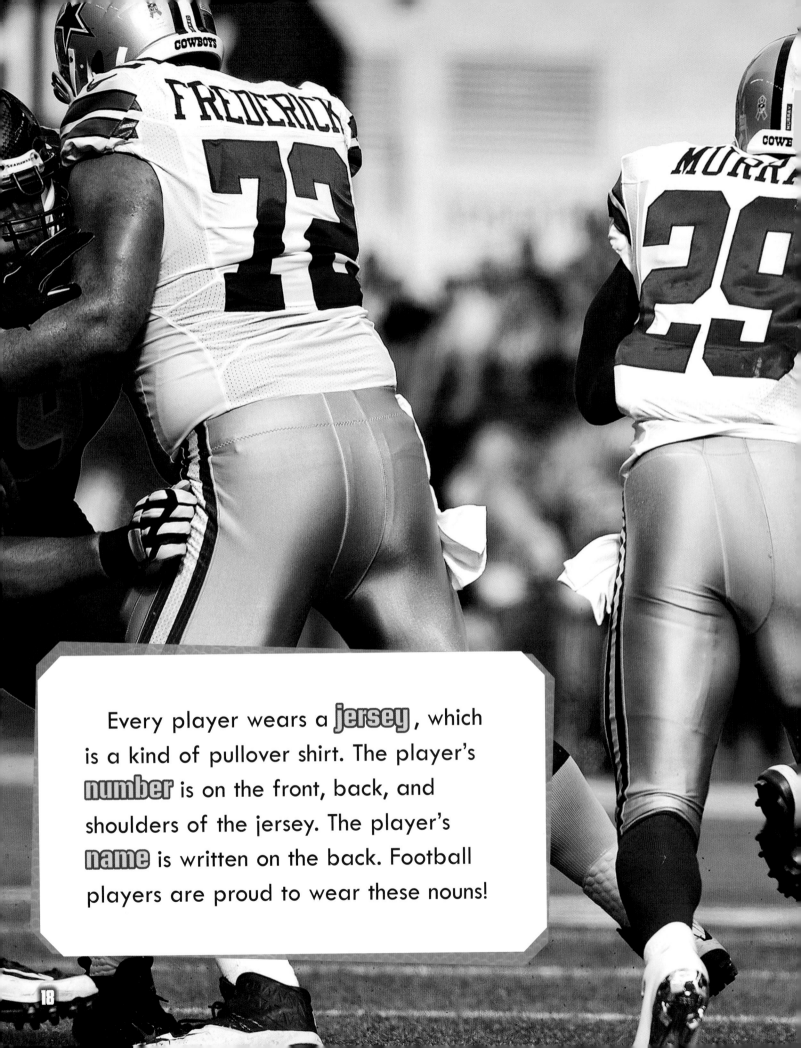

Every player wears a **jersey**, which is a kind of pullover shirt. The player's **number** is on the front, back, and shoulders of the jersey. The player's **name** is written on the back. Football players are proud to wear these nouns!

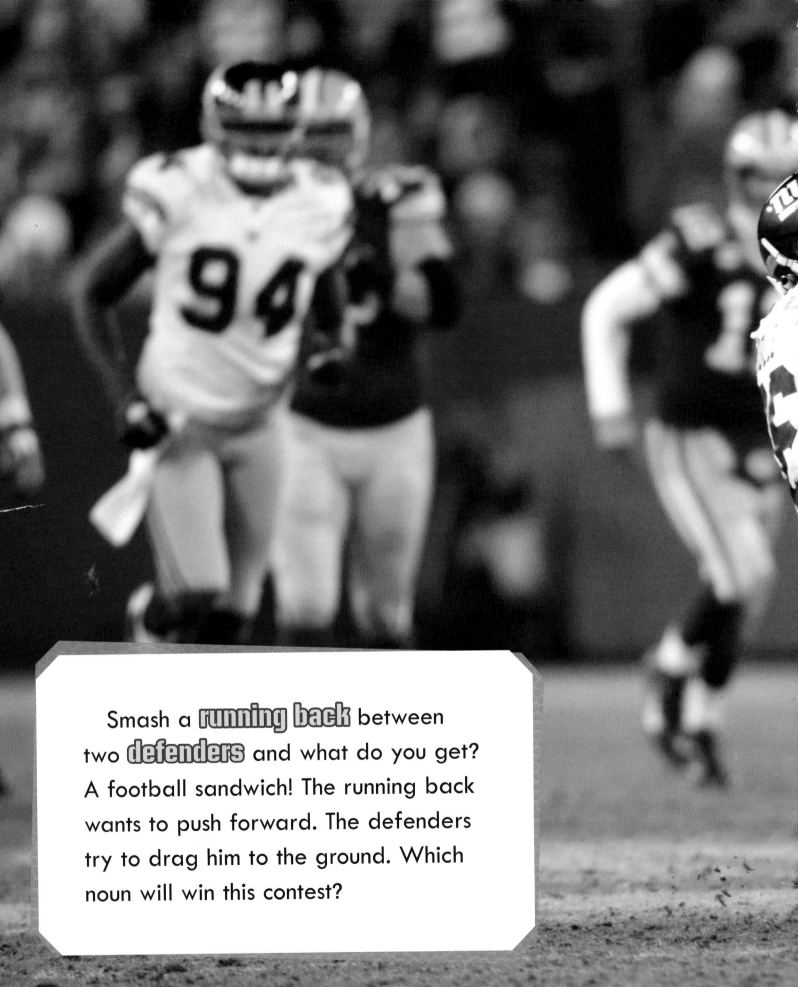

Smash a **running back** between two **defenders** and what do you get? A football sandwich! The running back wants to push forward. The defenders try to drag him to the ground. Which noun will win this contest?

During a break in the game, the team's **mascot** dashes onto the field. The mascot makes the crowd laugh and gets everyone excited. Some mascots bring special football nouns with them, like a giant **flag**.

A running back is only inches from the **end zone**. He drives forward with the ball, trying to carry it across the **goal line**. If he makes it, it's a **touchdown**. This noun will decide who wins the game!

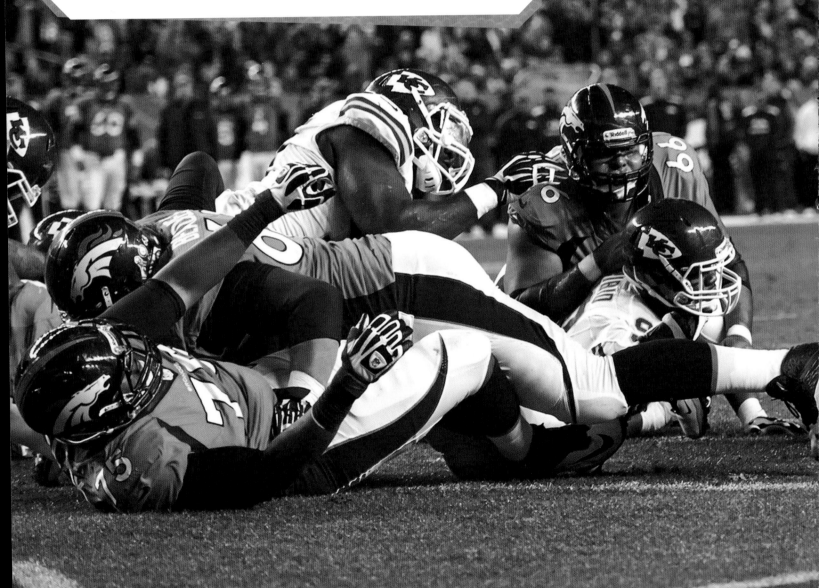

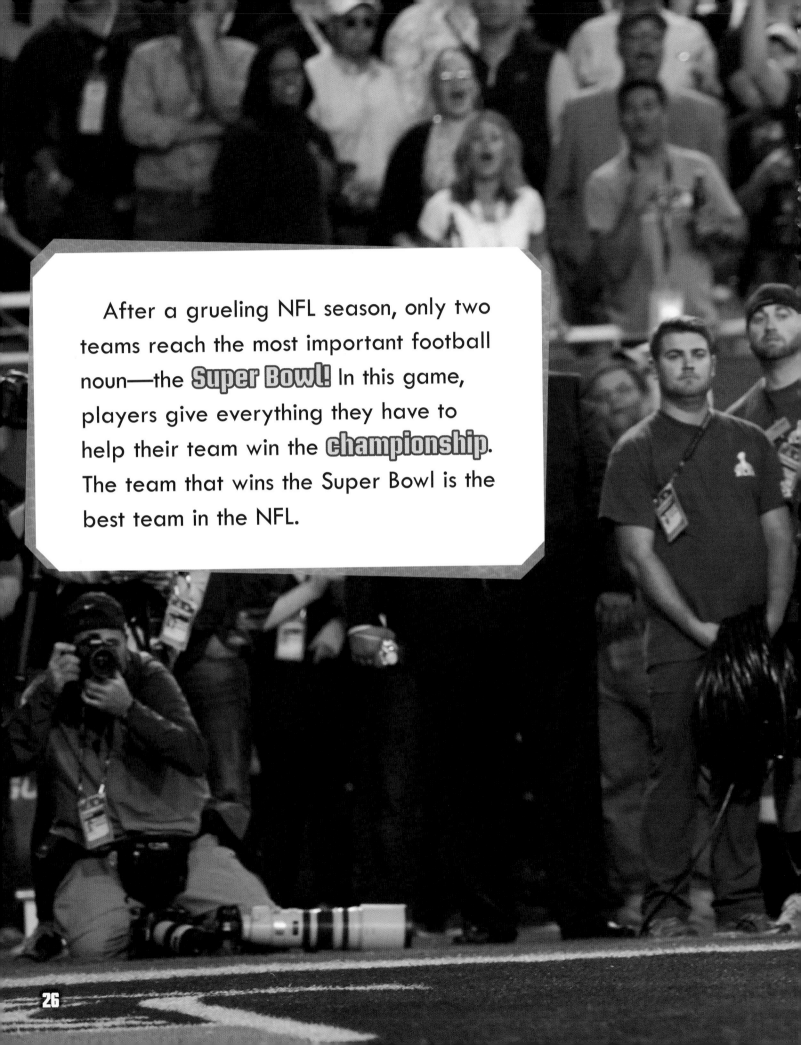

After a grueling NFL season, only two teams reach the most important football noun—the **Super Bowl!** In this game, players give everything they have to help their team win the **championship**. The team that wins the Super Bowl is the best team in the NFL.

What noun do football players like best? **Victory!** Find the nouns used in the following sentences that describe the exciting defensive touchdown.

In a stadium packed with fans, a defender returns an interception for a touchdown. Holding the football high, the player jumps for joy, and his shadow jumps too!

Answer: stadium, fans, defender, interception, touchdown, football, player, joy, shadow

GLOSSARY

captain (CAP-tuhn)—the leader of a sports team

coach (KOHCH)—a person who trains a sports team

defender (di-FEN-duhr)—a player on defense

end zone (END ZOHN)—the area between the goal line and the end line at either end of a football field

jersey (JUR-zee)—a sports shirt worn by athletes; jerseys often have the team name, last name, and number of the player

lineman (LINE-muhn)—player who specializes in play at the line of scrimmage

mascot (MASS-kot)—a person or animal that represents a sports team

stadium (STAY-dee-uhm)—a large building in which sports events are held

tee (TEE)—a stand that holds the football during a kickoff

touchdown (TUCH-down)—a six-point score in a football game

victory (VIK-tur-ee)—a win in a game or contest

READ MORE

Blaisdell, Bette. *A Pocket Full of Nouns.* Words I Know. North Mankato, Minn.: Capstone Press, 2014.

Cleary, Brian. *A Lime, A Mime, A Pool of Slime.* Words are CATegorical. New York: Millbrook Press, 2009.

Woop Studios. *A Zeal of Zebras: An Alphabet of Collective Nouns.* San Francisco: Chronicle Books, 2011.

INTERNET SITES

FactHound offers a safe, fun way to find Internet sites related to this book. All of the sites on FactHound have been researched by our staff.

Here's all you do:

Visit *www.facthound.com*

Type in this code: 9781620651742

Check out projects, games and lots more at
www.capstonekids.com

INDEX

Sports Illustrated Kids Football Words are published by Capstone Press,
1710 Roe Crest Drive, North Mankato, Minnesota 56003
www.capstonepub.com

Copyright © 2016 by Capstone Press, a Capstone imprint. All rights reserved.
No part of this publication may be reproduced in whole or in part, or stored in a
retrieval system, or transmitted in any form or by any means, electronic, mechanical,
photocopying, recording, or otherwise, without written permission of the publisher.

Sports Illustrated Kids is a trademark of Time Inc. Used with permission.

Library of Congress Cataloging-in-Publication Data
Cataloging-in-Publication data is on file with the Library of Congress.
ISBN 978-1-62065-174-2 (library binding)
ISBN 978-1-4914-7601-7 (eBook PDF)

Editorial Credits
Anthony Wacholtz, editor; Terri Poburka and Ted Williams, designers;
Eric Gohl, media researcher; Katy LaVigne, production specialist

Photo Credits
Sports Illustrated: Al Tielemans, cover, 1, 22–23, 26–27, Bill Frakes, 12–13, Damian
Strohmeyer, 20–21, David E. Klutho, 8–9, 10–11, John W. McDonough, 18–19, Peter
Read Miller, 2–3, Robert Beck, 4–5, 16–17, 24–25, Simon Bruty, 6–7, 14–15, 28–29

Design Elements: Shutterstock

Printed in the United States of America in North Mankato, Minnesota.
032015   008823CGF15